Learn Sass

Practical Guide

A. De Quattro

Copyright © 2024

Practical Guide

1.Introduction

Introduction to Sass

In recent years, web development has become increasingly complex and sophisticated, with a growing need to create more interactive and responsive user interfaces. CSS (Cascading Style Sheets) has been the go-to tool for defining the style and layout of web pages, but as web applications have grown more complex, plain CSS has begun to show its limitations. This is where Sass comes into play.

What is Sass?

Sass (Syntactically Awesome Style Sheets) is an extension of CSS that introduces advanced features for writing more powerful, flexible, and maintainable style sheets. Created by Hampton Catlin and Natalie Weizenbaum in 2006, Sass quickly became one of the most popular tools among front-end developers. It allows you to use variables, nesting, mixins, functions, extensions, and many other features not available in standard CSS.

Sass is a CSS preprocessor, meaning that Sass code is written in a separate language and then compiled into standard CSS before being used in the browser. This compilation process allows Sass to introduce syntax and features that would be impossible to implement directly in CSS. Additionally, Sass is backward-compatible with CSS, meaning that any valid CSS stylesheet is also a valid Sass stylesheet. This makes it very easy to integrate Sass into existing projects.

Sass is available in two main syntaxes: **SCSS (Sassy CSS)** and **Sass**. SCSS is the more modern and popular syntax and is fully compatible with traditional CSS syntax but with the added advanced features of Sass. The original Sass syntax is more concise, using indentation to define hierarchies instead of the braces and semicolons typical of CSS.

Both syntaxes offer the same features, and the choice between them mainly depends on personal preference or project standards.

Benefits of Using Sass

Adopting Sass brings a number of significant advantages over using plain CSS. These benefits translate into increased efficiency, maintainability, and organization of code, thereby improving the overall quality of the project.

1. **Variables**

One of the main advantages of Sass is the use of variables. Variables in Sass allow you to store values such as colors, font sizes, or spacing values that can be reused throughout the stylesheet. This not only makes the code more readable but also facilitates global changes: by changing the value of a variable, all elements using that variable will be updated automatically.

```scss
$primary-color: #3498db;
$font-stack: Helvetica, sans-serif;

body {
  font: 100% $font-stack;
  color: $primary-color;
}
```

2. **Nesting**

In CSS, nesting rules can become complicated and hard to manage, especially in large projects. Sass introduces a nesting mechanism that allows you to structure the code hierarchically, reflecting the underlying HTML structure. This makes the CSS code more readable and organized.

```scss
nav {
  ul {
    margin: 0;
    padding: 0;
    list-style: none;
  }

  li { display: inline-block; }

  a {
    text-decoration: none;
    color: $primary-color;

    &:hover {
      color: darken($primary-color, 10%);
```

```
      }
    }
  }
```

3. **Mixins**

Mixins in Sass allow you to define reusable blocks of code that can be included anywhere in the stylesheet. This is particularly useful for avoiding code repetition and efficiently managing CSS properties that require vendor prefixes, such as `transform`, `transition`, or `box-shadow`.

```scss
@mixin border-radius($radius) {
  -webkit-border-radius: $radius;
  -moz-border-radius: $radius;
  -ms-border-radius: $radius;
```

```
  border-radius: $radius;
}

.button {
  @include border-radius(10px);
}
```

4. **Partials and Import**

Sass allows you to split stylesheets into multiple partial files, which can be imported into a main file. This helps keep the code organized and modular. Partial files in Sass have a name that starts with an underscore (`_`), indicating that they should not be compiled directly into CSS but only when imported into another file.

```scss
```

```
// _reset.scss
* {
  margin: 0;
  padding: 0;
  box-sizing: border-box;
}


// styles.scss
@import 'reset';
@import 'typography';
@import 'layout';
```

5. **Functions**

Sass includes a number of built-in functions that allow you to manipulate values such as colors, numbers, and strings. For example, you can lighten or darken a color, calculate percentages, or manipulate strings. Additionally, you can define custom functions to extend Sass's capabilities further.

```scss
$base-color: #3498db;
$highlight-color: lighten($base-color, 20%);

.alert {
  background-color: $highlight-color;
  color: darken($base-color, 10%);
}
```

6. **Extensions**

Sass allows you to extend existing CSS rules using the `@extend` directive. This enables sharing properties between selectors without duplicating code. However, the use of

`@extend` should be managed carefully, as excessive use can result in more complex and harder-to-maintain CSS.

```scss
%button-styles {
  padding: 10px 20px;
  border: none;
  border-radius: 5px;
  display: inline-block;
  text-align: center;
}

.button-primary {
  @extend %button-styles;
  background-color: $primary-color;
  color: #fff;
}
```

```
.button-secondary {

  @extend %button-styles;

  background-color: darken($primary-color, 15%);

  color: #fff;

}
```

7. **Compatibility with CSS**

One of the strengths of Sass is its compatibility with CSS. Any valid CSS stylesheet can be a valid Sass stylesheet. This makes Sass extremely accessible for developers who already know CSS and want to gradually adopt Sass in their projects.

Installing Sass

Installing Sass is a relatively straightforward

process, and there are several methods available depending on your preferences and development environment. Below are the most common methods for installing Sass.

1. **Installing via npm (Node Package Manager)**

One of the most popular methods for installing Sass is via npm, the package manager for Node.js. This method is particularly useful if you are already using Node.js for your project.

First, make sure you have Node.js installed. You can download it from the official [Node.js](https://nodejs.org/) website.

Once Node.js is installed, you can install Sass by running the following command in your terminal:

```bash
npm install -g sass
```

The `-g` flag indicates that Sass will be installed globally, making it available for all projects on your system.

After installation, you can verify that Sass was installed correctly by running:

```bash
sass --version
```

This command will return the version of Sass installed, confirming that the installation was successful.

2. **Installing via Dart Sass**

Dart Sass is the official and most recent implementation of Sass, written in Dart. It is the recommended version for most users, as it offers the best performance and full compatibility with all Sass features.

You can install Dart Sass directly from the official [Sass](https://sass-lang.com/install) website or using precompiled packages for your operating system.

On macOS, you can install Dart Sass using Homebrew:

```bash
brew install sass/sass/sass
```

On Windows, you can download Dart Sass from the official website or use a PowerShell script for installation.

Once installed, you can compile your Sass files using the `sass` command:

```bash
sass input.scss output.css
```

3. **Installing via Ruby Sass (Obsolete)**

Ruby Sass was the original implementation of Sass but is now considered obsolete and is no longer maintained. It is recommended to use Dart Sass or another modern implementation. However, if you need to use Ruby Sass for some reason, you can install it via RubyGems:

```bash
gem install sass
```

```

However, since Ruby Sass is no longer supported, it is advisable to switch to Dart Sass or another more recent implementation.

#### 4. **Installing via Automation Scripts (Gulp, Webpack, etc.)**

If you are already using automation tools like Gulp, Webpack, or Grunt in your development workflow, you can easily integrate Sass into your build scripts.

For example, to use Sass with Gulp, you first need to install the necessary packages:

```bash
npm install gulp-sass sass --save-dev
```
```

Then, you can configure a Gulp task to compile your Sass files:

```javascript
const gulp = require('gulp');

const sass = require('gulp-sass')(require('sass'));

gulp.task('sass', function() {
  return gulp.src('./sass/**/*.scss')
    .pipe(sass().on('error', sass.logError))
    .pipe(gulp.dest('./css'));
});

gulp.task('watch', function() {
  gulp.watch('./sass/**/*.scss', gulp.series('sass'));
});
```

This task will compile all `.scss` files in the `sass` directory and save them in the `css` directory. The `watch` task will monitor changes to Sass files and automatically recompile the CSS.

5. **Using Sass Online**

If you want to try Sass without installing anything, there are several online tools that allow you to write and compile Sass code directly in the browser. Some examples include [SassMeister](https://www.sassmeister.com/) and [CodePen](https://codepen.io/), both of which offer interactive development environments for experimenting with Sass.

Sass is

a powerful tool that transforms the way developers write and manage stylesheets.

With advanced features like variables, nesting, mixins, and functions, Sass makes CSS more modular, reusable, and easier to maintain. Installing and integrating Sass into a project is simple and flexible, adapting easily to various workflows and development environments.

Adopting Sass can significantly improve productivity and code quality, making it an excellent choice for any front-end developer. Whether working on a small project or a large web application, Sass provides the tools needed to manage CSS more efficiently and professionally.

2. Basic Concepts

Sass (Syntactically Awesome Style Sheets) is one of the most popular and powerful CSS preprocessors used by front-end developers to enhance and organize their CSS code. Before diving into the specifics of Sass syntax and compilation, it is important to understand some basic concepts that form its foundation. In this section, we will explore the key concepts that distinguish Sass from CSS, the differences between Sass and SCSS syntax, and the methods of compilation.

Sass Syntax vs. CSS

Sass introduces an alternative syntax to traditional CSS, designed to make the process of writing CSS code more efficient and manageable. To fully understand the differences between Sass and CSS, it is helpful to examine how these two languages work and how Sass improves the web development workflow.

1. **Traditional CSS**

CSS (Cascading Style Sheets) is the standard language for defining the style and layout of web pages. Each CSS rule consists of a selector, which identifies the HTML element to which the rules apply, and a series of declarations enclosed in curly braces that specify the style properties to be applied.

A typical CSS rule example is as follows:

```css
body {
  font-family: Arial, sans-serif;
  background-color: #f0f0f0;
  color: #333;
}

h1 {
```

```
  font-size: 2em;

  color: #000;

}


p {

  line-height: 1.5;

  margin-bottom: 20px;

}
```

This syntax is simple and straightforward, but it has some limitations when it comes to managing complex and large stylesheets. For example, it does not support variables, functions, or significant nesting of rules.

2. **Sass Syntax**

Sass was created to overcome these limitations by introducing a more powerful and flexible syntax. The Sass syntax is designed to be more concise and readable compared to traditional CSS, removing the need for curly braces and semicolons.

An example of Sass code:

```sass
body
  font-family: Arial, sans-serif
  background-color: #f0f0f0
  color: #333

h1
  font-size: 2em
  color: #000

p
  line-height: 1.5
```

    margin-bottom: 20px
```

As you can see, in the Sass syntax:

- Curly braces are not used to delimit code blocks.

- Colons and semicolons are omitted.

- Indentation is used to indicate hierarchy between rules and declarations.

This cleaner and more minimalist syntax makes Sass code more readable and less prone to typos, especially in large projects.

#### 3. **SCSS Syntax**

In addition to the classic Sass syntax, there is a variant called SCSS (Sassy CSS), introduced in Sass version 3.0. SCSS is designed to be fully compatible with traditional CSS syntax but with the addition of all the advanced
```

features of Sass.

Here's the same code example written in SCSS:

```scss
body {
  font-family: Arial, sans-serif;
  background-color: #f0f0f0;
  color: #333;
}

h1 {
  font-size: 2em;
  color: #000;
}

p {
```

    line-height: 1.5;

    margin-bottom: 20px;

}
```

You'll notice that SCSS syntax is very similar to CSS, but it still supports all the advanced features of Sass, such as variables, mixins, and nesting.

#### 4. **Practical Differences Between Sass and CSS**

- **Reducing Redundancy:** Sass allows you to avoid code repetition by enabling the writing of more modular and maintainable styles.

- **Better Organization:** With the use of variables, mixins, and partials, Sass helps manage and organize code effectively.

- **Advanced Features:** Sass introduces
```

concepts such as nesting, inheritance, and functions that are not available in CSS.

Differences Between Sass and SCSS

A common question among those new to Sass is: What is the difference between Sass and SCSS? Although both are part of the same technology, there are some key differences worth understanding.

1. **Syntax**

The main difference between Sass and SCSS lies in the syntax.

- **Sass (Indented Syntax):** This is the original syntax and uses a format without curly braces and semicolons, relying instead on indentation to define hierarchies and structures in the code.

Example:

```sass
$primary-color: #3498db
body
  background-color: $primary-color
  font:
    family: Arial, sans-serif
    size: 14px
```

- **SCSS (Sassy CSS):** SCSS was introduced in Sass 3 and uses a syntax more similar to CSS. It retains curly braces and semicolons, making it easier for traditional CSS developers to transition to Sass without learning a new syntax.

Example:

```scss
```

```
$primary-color: #3498db;

body {
  background-color: $primary-color;
  font-family: Arial, sans-serif;
  font-size: 14px;
}
```

2. **CSS Compatibility**

- **SCSS:** Being designed as a superset of CSS, any valid CSS stylesheet is also a valid SCSS stylesheet. This means you can take an existing CSS file, rename it with the `.scss` extension, and continue working with it using Sass's advanced features.

- **Sass:** The indented syntax of Sass is not compatible with CSS. If you are working with Sass syntax and want to integrate CSS code, you will need to rewrite that code in the Sass syntax.

3. **Popularity and Preferences**

- **SCSS:** Today, SCSS is the most commonly used syntax for Sass. Its similarity to CSS makes it the preferred choice for most projects and developers.

- **Sass:** While the original Sass syntax has its proponents, it is less common compared to SCSS, partly because it requires a slightly steeper learning curve for those coming from plain CSS.

4. **File Extension**

- **Sass:** Files written with the Sass syntax must have the `.sass` extension.

- **SCSS:** Files written with the SCSS

syntax must have the `.scss` extension.

Compiling Sass

A fundamental concept of Sass is compilation. Since Sass is a preprocessor, files written in Sass or SCSS cannot be used directly in browsers. They need to be compiled into standard CSS before they can be linked to web pages. There are several methods and tools for compiling Sass into CSS, and here we will explore the most common ones.

1. **Manual Compilation via Command Line**

The most direct method for compiling Sass is through the command line, using the `sass` command to compile `.sass` or `.scss` files into CSS.

Example of compiling an SCSS file:

```bash
sass input.scss output.css
```

In this example:

- `input.scss` is the SCSS file to be compiled.

- `output.css` is the resulting CSS file.

You can also enable "watch" mode to automatically compile whenever the source file is modified:

```bash
sass --watch input.scss:output.css
```

This command continuously monitors the `input.scss` file and recompiles `output.css` whenever changes are made.

2. **Compiling with Gulp**

Gulp is a popular task runner used to automate development workflows. With Gulp, you can automate Sass compilation as part of your build process.

To get started, you need to install `gulp-sass` and Sass:

```bash
npm install gulp-sass sass --save-dev
```

Then, configure a Gulp task to compile Sass:

```javascript
const gulp = require('gulp');
const sass = require('gulp-sass')(require('sass'));
```

```
gulp.task('sass', function() {
  return gulp.src('./sass/**/*.scss')
    .pipe(sass().on('error', sass.logError))
    .pipe(gulp.dest('./css'));
});


gulp.task('watch', function() {
  gulp.watch('./sass/**/*.scss', gulp.series('sass'));
});
```

With this setup, whenever you modify an `.scss` file in the `sass` directory, Gulp will automatically recompile the CSS.

3. **Compiling with Webpack**

Webpack is a powerful module bundler that

can be used to manage Sass as part of the build pipeline. To use Sass with Webpack, you need to install some specific loaders:

```bash
npm install sass-loader sass style-loader css-loader --save-dev
```

Then, configure the `webpack.config.js` file to include Sass:

```javascript
module.exports = {
  module: {
    rules: [
      {
        test: /\.scss$/,
        use: [
          'style-loader',
```

```
            'css-loader',
            'sass-loader'
          ]
        }
      ]
    }
};
```

With this configuration, Webpack will handle the compilation of `.scss` files into CSS and inject them directly into the page during development.

4. **Automatic Compilation with Text Editors**

Many modern text editors, such as Visual Studio Code, Atom, and Sublime Text, offer plugins or packages for automatic Sass compilation. These tools significantly streamline the workflow, allowing you to write Sass code and see it compiled into CSS immediately.

For example, in Visual Studio Code, you can use the **Live Sass Compiler** extension:

1. Install the **Live Sass Compiler** extension from the Visual Studio Code marketplace.

2. Open your `.scss` file.

3. Click the "Watch Sass" button at the bottom right.

This will automatically compile `.scss` files every time they are saved.

5. **Compilation with Frameworks**

Many CSS frameworks, such as Bootstrap and

Foundation, use Sass for their configurability and modularity. When working with these frameworks, Sass compilation is often integrated into their build system.

For instance, when you download a customized version of Bootstrap, you can configure Sass variables in the `_variables.scss` file and compile it into CSS using the methods described above (Gulp, Webpack, command line, etc.).

6. **Online Compilation**

If you prefer to avoid installing local tools, you can also use online Sass compilers. Tools like [SassMeister](https://www.sassmeister.com/) offer an interactive development environment in the browser, where you can write Sass code and see the compiled CSS in real-time.

7. **Compilation and Optimization**

Sass compilation can be combined with other optimizations, such as minification and autoprefixing.

- **Minification:** After compilation, CSS can be minified to reduce file size and improve load times. This can be done using tools like `cssnano` or the `--style compressed` option with the `sass` command.

```bash
sass --style compressed input.scss output.min.css
```

- **Autoprefixing:** Since different browsers support CSS properties differently, it is often necessary to add vendor-specific prefixes (e.g., `-webkit-`, `-moz-`, etc.). This can be automated using tools like `Autoprefixer`, which analyzes the compiled CSS and adds the necessary prefixes.

An example using Gulp:

```javascript
const gulp = require('gulp');
const sass = require('gulp-sass')(require('sass'));
const autoprefixer = require('gulp-autoprefixer');

gulp.task('sass', function() {
  return gulp.src('./sass/**/*.scss')
    .pipe(sass({ outputStyle: 'compressed' }).on('error', sass.logError))
    .pipe(autoprefixer({
      overrideBrowserslist: ['last 2 versions'],
      cascade: false
```

```
    }))

    .pipe(gulp.dest('./css'));
  });
```

In this way, the final CSS will be not only minified but also compatible with major browsers.

Adopting Sass in your web development process can completely transform the way stylesheets are written and managed. With features like variables, nesting, mixins, and modular code organization, Sass offers a level of flexibility and power that goes far beyond what is possible with CSS alone. The choice between Sass and SCSS largely depends on personal preference and project needs, but both syntaxes provide powerful tools to enhance productivity and code quality.

Finally, compiling Sass is an essential step that can be done in various ways depending on your workflow and tools. Whether you prefer a manual setup, a task runner like Gulp, a bundler like Webpack, or even an online compiler, the key is to leverage Sass's capabilities to create well-organized, efficient, and maintainable stylesheets.

3. Variables in Sass

Variables in Sass are one of the key tools that make this CSS preprocessor so powerful and versatile. They allow you to store values that can be reused throughout your code, simplifying maintenance, improving consistency, and making your CSS more modular. Variables can hold values of various types, such as colors, fonts, sizes, numbers, and strings, and can be used for any CSS property.

Introduction to Sass Variables

In traditional CSS, whenever you need to use the same value (e.g., a color or a size) in multiple places within the stylesheet, you have to repeat that value in every single declaration. This leads to redundant code that is difficult to update. Sass variables solve this problem by allowing you to define a value once and reuse it throughout your code.

Here's a basic example of using variables in Sass:

```scss
$primary-color: #3498db;
$font-stack: 'Helvetica Neue', sans-serif;

body {
  font-family: $font-stack;
  color: $primary-color;
}

h1 {
  color: $primary-color;
}
```

In this example, the `$primary-color` variable holds a hexadecimal color, and the `$font-stack` variable contains a list of fonts. These variables are then used in multiple declarations within the stylesheet, reducing code repetition and making it easy to modify these values in one place.

Creating and Using Variables

1. **Declaring a Variable**

Declaring a variable in Sass is straightforward. By using the `$` symbol followed by the variable name, you can assign any value to a variable. The general syntax for declaring a variable is:

```scss
$variable-name: value;
```

For example:

```scss
$primary-color: #3498db;

$font-size: 16px;
```

Once declared, a variable can be used anywhere in the stylesheet.

2. **Using Variables**

Variables in Sass can be used anywhere in the code. For instance, you can use them to define colors, sizes, fonts, margins, padding, and any other CSS property.

Example:

```scss
```

```
$padding-large: 20px;

$border-color: #e74c3c;


.container {

  padding: $padding-large;

  border: 1px solid $border-color;

}
```

In this case, `$padding-large` and `$border-color` are used to define the padding and border color of a container.

3. **Updating Variable Values**

One of the main advantages of variables is the ease with which you can update values across the entire stylesheet. For example, if you decide to change the primary color of the site, you just need to modify the value of the

`$primary-color` variable, and the change will be reflected everywhere that variable is used.

```scss
$primary-color: #2ecc71; // Change the primary color

h1 {
  color: $primary-color; // Automatically updated with the new color
}
```

4. **Advanced Variable Usage**

Variables in Sass can be combined with other advanced features, such as mixins, functions, and arithmetic operations.

Example of variables with mixins:

```scss
@mixin button($bg-color, $font-color) {
  background-color: $bg-color;
  color: $font-color;
  padding: 10px 20px;
  border-radius: 5px;
}

.button-primary {
  @include button($primary-color, #fff);
}
```

In this example, the `button` mixin uses variables to make the code more modular and reusable.

**Example of arithmetic operations with

variables:**

```scss
$base-font-size: 16px;
$line-height: 1.5;
$base-line-height: $base-font-size * $line-height;

body {
  font-size: $base-font-size;
  line-height: $base-line-height;
}
```

In this case, variables are used in arithmetic operations to automatically calculate the `line-height` value.

Data Types in Variables

Variables in Sass can hold different types of data. These include numbers, strings, colors, lists, maps, and boolean values. Understanding the various data types available in Sass allows you to fully leverage its capabilities.

1. **Numbers**

Numbers in Sass can represent any numeric value, such as dimensions, widths, heights, margins, padding, etc. Numbers can have units (like `px`, `%`, `em`, etc.) or can be simple integers or decimals.

Examples:

```scss
$base-width: 100px;

$padding-top: 20px;

$line-height: 1.5;
```

```

You can also perform arithmetic operations on numbers:

```scss
$double-padding: $padding-top * 2;
```

2. **Strings**

Strings are sequences of characters enclosed in single or double quotes. Strings can be used to represent values like fonts, URLs, class names, etc.

Examples:

```scss

```scss
$font-family: 'Helvetica Neue', sans-serif;
$bg-image: 'url("background.jpg")';
```

Strings can be concatenated using the `+` operator:

```scss
$full-url: 'url("' + $bg-image + '")';
```

3. **Colors**

Sass supports colors in various formats, such as hexadecimal (`#3498db`), color names (`red`), RGB values (`rgb(52, 152, 219)`), and HSL values (`hsl(207, 100%, 50%)`). Colors can be manipulated using Sass's built-in functions to lighten, darken, saturate, or desaturate a color, among other things.

Examples:

```scss
$primary-color: #3498db;
$secondary-color: lighten($primary-color, 10%);
```

In this example, `$secondary-color` is a lighter version of the primary color.

4. **Lists**

Lists in Sass are ordered sequences of values, separated by spaces or commas. Lists are useful for representing groups of values, like a list of fonts or a series of dimensions.

Examples:

```scss
$font-stack: 'Helvetica', 'Arial', sans-serif;
$dimensions: 10px 20px 30px 40px;
```

Lists can be iterated using directives like `@each`:

```scss
@each $color in red, green, blue {
  .text-#{$color} {
    color: $color;
  }
}
```

This code will generate `.text-red`, `.text-green`, `.text-blue` classes with the respective colors.

5. **Maps**

Maps in Sass are data structures that contain key-value pairs. They are similar to objects in JavaScript or dictionaries in Python and can be used to represent more complex data sets.

Examples:

```scss
$colors: (
  primary: #3498db,
  secondary: #2ecc71,
  danger: #e74c3c
);

.button {
```

      background-color: map-get($colors, primary);

}
```

You can use the `map-get` function to retrieve a value from a map based on its key.

#### 6. **Booleans**

Boolean values in Sass can be `true` or `false`. These values are often used in conditions (`if`, `else`) to control the flow of the code.

Examples:

```scss
$feature-enabled: true;

```
@if $feature-enabled {
  .feature {
    display: block;
  }
} @else {
  .feature {
    display: none;
  }
}
```

In this case, the `.feature` class will be displayed only if `$feature-enabled` is `true`.

Scoped Variables

One of the more advanced aspects of variables in Sass is the concept of "scoped variables," meaning variables with specific scopes. In

Sass, variables can have either global or local scope, depending on where they are declared.

1. **Global Scope**

Variables declared outside of any code block (like mixins or functions) have a global scope. This means they can be accessed and used anywhere in the stylesheet.

Example:

```scss
$global-color: #3498db;

body {
  color: $global-color;
}
```

In this example, `$global-color` is a global variable and can be used anywhere in the code.

2. **Local Scope**

Variables can be declared inside code blocks, such as mixins, functions, or nested blocks. These variables have a local scope and are only accessible within the block where they are declared.

Example:

```scss
@mixin theme($primary-color) {
  $text-color: darken($primary-color, 20%);
  color: $text-color;
}
```

```scss
.button {
  @include theme(#3498db);
}
```

In this example, the `$text-color` variable is declared within the `theme` mixin, so it has a local scope to that mixin. This means that `$text-color` is not accessible outside of the mixin and can only be used within it. When the mixin is included in the `.button` class, the `$primary-color` variable is passed as a parameter, and the text color is calculated based on that variable.

3. **Variable Shadowing**

In Sass, it is possible to have variables with the same name both globally and locally. When a local variable has the same name as a global variable, the local variable "shadows" (or "hides") the global variable within its scope. This phenomenon is known as "shadowing."

Example:

```scss
$color: #e74c3c; // Global variable

@mixin theme($primary-color) {
  $color: darken($primary-color, 20%); // Local variable that shadows the global one
  color: $color;
}

.button {
  @include theme(#3498db); // The local $color variable is used here
}
```

```
p {
    color: $color; // The global $color variable is used here
}
```

In this example, the global `$color` variable is defined at the top, but within the `theme` mixin, a local `$color` variable is declared. This local variable shadows the global one within the mixin, so when the mixin is included in the `.button` class, the local `$color` variable is used. Outside the mixin, however, the global `$color` variable is used.

4. **Default Values with `!default`**

Sass allows you to set default values for variables using the `!default` flag. This flag tells Sass to assign a value to a variable only if that variable hasn't been assigned a value before. This feature is particularly useful when building reusable components or libraries.

Example:

```scss
$primary-color: #3498db !default;

.button {
  background-color: $primary-color;
}
```

If `$primary-color` has already been assigned a value earlier in the code, the `!default` assignment will not override that value. However, if `$primary-color` is not defined anywhere else, it will be set to `#3498db`.

Variables in Sass significantly enhance the

way you write and maintain CSS by promoting code reusability, reducing repetition, and making it easier to apply consistent styles across your projects. Whether you are handling simple color definitions or complex maps, Sass variables provide the flexibility and power you need to manage your styles effectively.

By understanding the different types of variables and how to use them within various scopes, you can create more efficient, maintainable, and scalable stylesheets. The next step is to dive deeper into advanced Sass features, like mixins, functions, and control directives, to take full advantage of what Sass has to offer in your development workflow.

4. Nesting, Mixins in Sass

The concept of "nesting" in Sass is one of the most appreciated features of this preprocessor, as it mirrors the natural structure of HTML markup, making CSS more readable and organized. Nesting allows you to nest selectors within other selectors, reflecting the hierarchy of HTML elements. In other words, it lets you write CSS so that more specific selectors are nested under more general ones, facilitating the readability and maintenance of the code.

Example of Selector Nesting

Let's consider a simple HTML markup example:

```html
<div class="nav">
  <ul>
```

```html
    <li><a href="#">Home</a></li>
    <li><a href="#">About</a></li>
    <li><a href="#">Contact</a></li>
  </ul>
</div>
```

Writing CSS for this markup in a standard CSS file might look like this:

```css
.nav {
  background-color: #333;
}

.nav ul {
  list-style-type: none;
}
```

```
.nav ul li {
  display: inline-block;
}

.nav ul li a {
  color: white;
  text-decoration: none;
}
```

While this approach is correct, it can quickly become complex and difficult to maintain as the HTML structure gets deeper or more intricate. Using nesting in Sass, we can rewrite the same code in a much more readable way:

```scss
.nav {
```

```
  background-color: #333;

  ul {
    list-style-type: none;

    li {
      display: inline-block;

      a {
        color: white;
        text-decoration: none;
      }
    }
  }
}
```

In this example, the `ul`, `li`, and `a` selectors are nested inside the `.nav` selector, visually reflecting the HTML structure. This makes it immediately clear that these styles are applied to descendants of `.nav`, improving the readability and organization of the code.

Nesting Pseudo-Classes and Pseudo-Elements

Nesting in Sass is not limited to standard selectors; it also extends to pseudo-classes and pseudo-elements. Here's an example:

```scss
button {
  background-color: #3498db;
  color: white;

  &:hover {
    background-color: #2980b9;
  }
```

```
  &::before {
    content: '→';
    margin-right: 10px;
  }
}
```

In this case, using `&:hover` and `&::before` allows you to handle states and pseudo-elements within the context of the `button` selector, further enhancing the clarity of the code.

Nesting Limits and Best Practices

While nesting is a powerful Sass feature, it's important to use it judiciously to avoid creating complex and hard-to-manage CSS. Here are some limits and best practices to consider when using nesting:

1. **Nesting Depth**

Although Sass allows you to nest selectors to any depth, it's advisable to keep nesting as shallow as possible. A good rule of thumb is to limit nesting to three levels deep. Excessive nesting can lead to over-specified CSS, which is not only difficult to read and maintain but can also negatively impact browser performance.

Example of excessive nesting:

```scss
.container {
  .nav {
    ul {
      li {
        a {
          span {
```

```
      color: red;
    }
   }
  }
 }
}
}
```

This kind of code should be avoided, as it is difficult to follow and can result in overly specific CSS selectors that are hard to override.

2. **Avoid Unnecessary Class Nesting**

A common mistake is nesting classes that don't benefit from it, just for the sake of nesting. For example, if a class can be defined independently without ambiguity, there's no need to nest it within another selector.

Example to avoid:

```scss
.nav {
  .header {
    color: blue;
  }
}
```

In this case, `.header` could be defined separately if there is no strong hierarchical relationship with `.nav`.

3. **Use Nesting to Enhance Consistency**

Nesting is useful for creating modular CSS, where related blocks of code are kept together. This helps ensure that changes to a specific part of the interface are easy to track and manage.

Example of good nesting use:

```scss
.card {
  border: 1px solid #ddd;
  padding: 20px;

  .card-title {
    font-size: 1.5em;
    margin-bottom: 10px;
  }

  .card-content {
    font-size: 1em;
    color: #333;
  }
```

```
}
```

Here, the `.card-title` and `.card-content` selectors are clearly associated with the context of the `.card`, improving the modularity and consistency of the code.

Mixins in Sass

What is a Mixin?

A mixin in Sass is a reusable function that allows you to encapsulate and reuse blocks of CSS code dynamically. Unlike variables, which store single values, mixins can contain entire blocks of CSS declarations, including selectors, properties, and even directives like media queries. Mixins are ideal for avoiding code repetition and managing complex styles that need to be applied in multiple places in the stylesheet.

Example of a Simple Mixin

A classic example of a mixin is one used to create buttons:

```scss
@mixin button-styles {
  background-color: #3498db;
  color: white;
  padding: 10px 20px;
  border-radius: 5px;
  text-transform: uppercase;
}

.button {
  @include button-styles;
}
```

In this example, the `button-styles` mixin contains all the CSS declarations necessary to style a button. By using `@include`, we can apply this mixin to any `.button` class in the stylesheet. If we needed to create another type of button, we could simply include the mixin again without having to rewrite all the code.

Creating and Using Mixins

Mixins are created using the `@mixin` directive, followed by the mixin's name and a block of code that encloses the CSS declarations. To use a mixin, the `@include` directive is used, followed by the mixin's name.

Creating a Mixin

To create a mixin, follow this syntax:

```scss
```

```
@mixin mixin-name {
  // CSS declarations
}
```

Here's a practical example:

```scss
@mixin rounded-corners {
  border-radius: 10px;
  -webkit-border-radius: 10px; // For older browser support
  -moz-border-radius: 10px;    // For older browser support
}
```

Including a Mixin

Once a mixin is created, you can include it in any CSS rule using `@include`:

```scss
.box {
  @include rounded-corners;
  background-color: #eee;
}
```

This will apply the declarations contained in the `rounded-corners` mixin to the `.box` class.

Passing Parameters to Mixins

Mixins in Sass become particularly powerful when you can pass parameters. Parameters allow you to create flexible and reusable mixins that can be customized each time they are included.

Example of a Mixin with Parameters

Here's how you can extend our `button-styles` mixin example to accept parameters:

```scss
@mixin button-styles($bg-color, $font-color) {
  background-color: $bg-color;
  color: $font-color;
  padding: 10px 20px;
  border-radius: 5px;
  text-transform: uppercase;
}

.button-primary {
  @include button-styles(#3498db, white);
```

```
}


.button-secondary {

  @include button-styles(#2ecc71, white);

}
```

In this example, `button-styles` accepts two parameters: `$bg-color` and `$font-color`. This allows us to create different button variants by simply changing the parameter values.

Parameters with Default Values

Another useful feature of Sass mixins is the ability to define default values for parameters. This allows you to call a mixin without having to pass all the parameters every time, only those you want to customize.

Example:

```scss
@mixin button-styles($bg-color: #3498db, $font-color: white) {
  background-color: $bg-color;
  color: $font-color;
  padding: 10px 20px;
  border-radius: 5px;
  text-transform: uppercase;
}

.button {
  @include button-styles; // Uses default values
}

.button-custom {
  @include button-styles(#e74c3c, #fff); // Uses custom values
```

}
```

In this case, if `button-styles` is included without passing parameters, the default values (`#3498db` for the background and `white` for the text) will be used. However, if you want to customize one or both values, you can pass them directly to the mixin when including it.

Using nesting and mixins in Sass represents a significant improvement over writing traditional CSS. These features not only enhance the readability and maintainability of the code but also allow for more modular and reusable CSS.

Nesting allows you to structure your CSS code to reflect the hierarchy of HTML markup, reducing the need for repetition and improving code consistency. However, it is essential to follow best practices to avoid
```

excessive nesting, which could lead to over-specification and unnecessary complexity.

Mixins, on the other hand, offer a powerful way to encapsulate reusable blocks of CSS code, with the added flexibility of passing parameters and defining default values. This makes the development process more efficient and the final code cleaner and more modular.

By combining these techniques, designers and developers can create CSS stylesheets

that are not only easier to maintain but also more powerful and flexible, facilitating the creation of complex and consistent user interfaces.

5. Functions and Operators

Functions in Sass are powerful tools that enable writing more dynamic and modular CSS code. Sass functions fall into two main categories: built-in functions and custom functions. In addition, it is crucial to understand how these functions can be used within variables and mixins, as well as how mathematical and comparison operators can be used to manipulate data in Sass.

Sass Built-in Functions

Sass provides a range of built-in functions that make it easier to manipulate colors, sizes, and other CSS units. These functions are extremely useful for applying transformations and calculations directly within your CSS.

Examples of Built-in Functions

1. **Color Manipulation**

   - `lighten($color, $amount)`: Lightens a color by a specified amount.

   - `darken($color, $amount)`: Darkens a color by a specified amount.

   - `saturate($color, $amount)`: Increases the saturation of a color.

   - `desaturate($color, $amount)`: Decreases the saturation of a color.

   - `mix($color1, $color2, $weight)`: Mixes two colors with a specified weight.

   Example of usage:

   ```scss
   $base-color: #3498db;

   .button {
       background-color: lighten($base-color,
   ```

20%);

color: darken($base-color, 30%);

}
```

2. **Size Calculations**

- `px()`, `em()`, `rem()`: Convert values to different units of measurement.

- `percentage($value)`: Converts a value into a percentage.

Example:

```scss
$container-width: 960px;

.content {
    width: percentage(0.75); // Converted to

percentage

```
max-width: $container-width;
}
```

3. **String Functions**

- `str-length($string)`: Returns the length of a string.

- `str-insert($string, $insert, $index)`: Inserts a string into another string at a specified position.

- `str-slice($string, $start, $end)`: Extracts a part of the string.

Example:

```scss
$text: "Hello, World!";
```

```
.greeting {
  content: str-slice($text, 1, 5); // Returns "Hello"
}
```

Creating Custom Functions

In Sass, you can create custom functions to perform specific calculations and manipulations, further enhancing the modularity and reusability of your code. Custom functions are declared using the `@function` directive and can accept parameters and return values.

Basic Syntax for Creating Functions

```scss
```

```
@function function-name($parameter) {
  @return value;
}
```

Example of a Custom Function

Suppose you want to create a function that calculates the width of a column based on a percentage of the container.

```scss
@function column-width($columns, $total-columns: 12) {
  @return ($columns / $total-columns) * 100%;
}

.column-6 {
```

```
  width: column-width(6); // Returns 50%
}
```

In this example, the `column-width` function calculates the width of a column as a percentage of the total columns. By passing `6` as a parameter, we get a width of 50%.

Using Functions in Variables and Mixins

Functions can be used within variables and mixins to generate dynamic and customized values. This allows you to keep your CSS code modular and easily updatable.

Example of a Function in Variables

```scss
```

```scss
@function border-radius($radius) {
  @return $radius * 1px;
}

$base-radius: border-radius(10);

.box {
  border-radius: $base-radius; // Result: 10px
}
```

Example of a Function in Mixins

```scss
@mixin box-shadow($offset-x, $offset-y, $blur-radius, $color) {
  box-shadow: $offset-x $offset-y $blur-radius $color;
}
```

```
.box {
  @include box-shadow(0, 4px, 8px, rgba(0, 0, 0, 0.2));
}
```

In this example, the `box-shadow` mixin uses parameters to define the offsets, blur radius, and color of the shadow. These parameters can be passed when the mixin is included.

Operators in Sass

Operators in Sass are used to perform mathematical and comparison operations on values. These operators allow you to manipulate and calculate values directly within the stylesheet.

Mathematical Operators

Mathematical operators in Sass include:

- `+` (Addition): Adds two values.

- `-` (Subtraction): Subtracts one value from another.

- `*` (Multiplication): Multiplies two values.

- `/` (Division): Divides one value by another.

Example of Mathematical Operators

```scss
$base-size: 16px;
$padding: $base-size * 2; // 32px
$margin: $padding / 2;   // 16px

.container {
  padding: $padding;
  margin: $margin;
```

}
```

In this example, mathematical operators are used to calculate the padding and margin of a container based on the base size.

#### Comparison Operators

Comparison operators in Sass include:

- `==` (Equal to): Checks if two values are equal.

- `!=` (Not equal to): Checks if two values are not equal.

- `>` (Greater than): Checks if one value is greater than another.

- `<` (Less than): Checks if one value is less than another.

- `>=` (Greater than or equal to): Checks if
```

one value is greater than or equal to another.

- `<=` (Less than or equal to): Checks if one value is less than or equal to another.

Example of Comparison Operators

```scss
$width: 100px;

.container {
  @if $width > 50px {
    width: $width;
  } @else {
    width: 50px;
  }
}
```

In this example, the comparison operator `>` is used to check if `$width` is greater than `50px`. Depending on the result of the comparison, a different width value is applied.

Using Operators in Sass

Operators can be used not only for mathematical calculations and comparisons but also to combine these results with other CSS properties. This allows for the creation of dynamic and responsive styles.

Example of Using Operators

```scss
$base-color: #3498db;
$darken-factor: 10%;

.button {
```

```
background-color: $base-color;

&:hover {

  background-color: darken($base-color, $darken-factor);

}

}
```
```

In this example, the `darken` function is used together with a variable to create a dynamic color variation for the hover state.

### Inheritance (Extend) in Sass

Inheritance in Sass, managed through the `@extend` directive, allows you to share styles between selectors without duplicating code. This improves modularity and reduces code repetition in CSS.
```

How `@extend` Works

The `@extend` directive allows one selector to extend another selector, inheriting its CSS declarations. When used, Sass copies all rules from the extended selector to the current selector.

Example of Using `@extend`

```scss
%base-button {
  display: inline-block;
  padding: 10px 20px;
  border-radius: 5px;
  text-align: center;
}

.button-primary {
```

    @extend %base-button;
    background-color: #3498db;
    color: white;
}

.button-secondary {
    @extend %base-button;
    background-color: #2ecc71;
    color: white;
}
```

In this example, the `%base-button` selector is a placeholder (intermediate selector) containing shared styles. The `.button-primary` and `.button-secondary` classes extend `%base-button`, inheriting all its declarations and adding specific styles.

#### Advantages of Using `@extend`
```

1. **Reduction of Repetition**: Helps avoid duplicating common CSS rules between multiple selectors.

2. **Improved Maintenance**: Facilitates centralized modification of shared styles. Changing the `%base-button` placeholder automatically reflects in all selectors that extend it.

3. **Performance Improvement**: Generates more optimized CSS by reducing the number of duplicated rules in the resulting CSS file.

Limitations of `@extend`

1. **Specificity**: `@extend` can affect the specificity of the resulting CSS, which can lead to overwriting issues if not managed properly.

2. **Scalability**: Excessive use of `@extend` can result in less predictable and harder-to-debug CSS. It's important to use `@extend` carefully and prefer mixins and other techniques for complex cases.

In Sass, functions, operators, and inheritance are fundamental tools for writing efficient, modular, and reusable CSS code. Built-in and custom functions allow for dynamic value manipulation and calculation, while operators facilitate mathematical operations and comparisons. Inheritance (`@extend`) helps reduce code repetition and improve CSS maintenance.

By effectively using these tools, designers and developers can create more robust and manageable stylesheets, simplifying the creation of complex user interfaces and optimizing the CSS development process.

6. Lists and Maps in Sass, and @import and @use

Lists and maps in Sass are advanced data structures that enable efficient and dynamic management of collections of values. These structures are particularly useful for organizing data and applying complex styles without duplicating code. Below, we will explore in detail how to create and use lists and maps in Sass, as well as how to iterate over them.

Creating and Using Lists

Lists in Sass are similar to arrays in other programming languages. They can contain values of any type and can be used to manage collections of data.

Creating Lists

Lists are created by enclosing values in parentheses and separating them with commas:

```scss
$colors: (red, green, blue);
$sizes: (12px, 16px, 20px);
```

In this example, `$colors` is a list containing three colors, and `$sizes` is a list containing three sizes.

Accessing List Elements

To access a specific element in a list, you use the `nth()` function:

```scss
$primary-color: nth($colors, 1); // red
```

```
$font-size: nth($sizes, 2); // 16px
```

In this example, `nth($colors, 1)` returns the first element of the `$colors` list, which is `red`. Similarly, `nth($sizes, 2)` returns the second element of the `$sizes` list, which is `16px`.

Adding and Removing List Elements

Lists can be manipulated using functions like `append()` and `remove()`:

```scss
$new-colors: append($colors, yellow); // (red, green, blue, yellow)

$updated-colors: remove($new-colors, 2); // (red, blue, yellow)
```

In this example, `append($colors, yellow)` adds `yellow` to the `$colors` list, while `remove($new-colors, 2)` removes the second element from the `$new-colors` list.

Iterating Over Lists

Sass doesn't directly support traditional `for` loops like other programming languages, but you can iterate over lists using the `@each` directive:

```scss
@each $color in $colors {
  .text-#{$color} {
    color: $color;
  }
}
```

In this example, `@each` iterates through the

`$colors` list and creates a class for each color, such as `.text-red`, `.text-green`, and `.text-blue`, applying the corresponding color.

Creating and Using Maps

Maps in Sass are similar to objects in JavaScript or dictionaries in Python. They allow you to associate keys with values, which is useful for managing structured data.

Creating Maps

Maps are created using curly braces, with keys and values separated by colons:

```scss
$theme-colors: (
  primary: #3498db,
  secondary: #2ecc71,
```

    danger: #e74c3c

);

$font-sizes: (

  small: 12px,

  medium: 16px,

  large: 20px

);
```

In this example, `$theme-colors` is a map associating color names with color values, and `$font-sizes` associates size names with font sizes.

##### Accessing Map Values

To access values within a map, you use the `map-get()` function:
```

```scss
$primary-color: map-get($theme-colors, primary); // #3498db

$medium-font-size: map-get($font-sizes, medium); // 16px
```

In this example, `map-get($theme-colors, primary)` returns the value associated with the `primary` key in the `$theme-colors` map, which is `#3498db`. Similarly, `map-get($font-sizes, medium)` returns `16px`.

Modifying Maps

Maps can be modified using functions like `map-merge()` and `map-remove()`:

```scss
$extended-theme-colors: map-merge($theme-colors, (
```

```
  info: #3498db
)); // (primary: #3498db, secondary: #2ecc71, danger: #e74c3c, info: #3498db)

$theme-without-danger: map-remove($theme-colors, danger); // (primary: #3498db, secondary: #2ecc71)
```

In this example, `map-merge($theme-colors, (info: #3498db))` adds a new `info` key to the `$theme-colors` map, while `map-remove($theme-colors, danger)` removes the `danger` key.

Iterating Over Maps

To iterate over maps, you use the `@each` directive with a slightly different syntax:

```scss
```

```
@each $name, $color in $theme-colors {
  .bg-#{$name} {
    background-color: $color;
  }
}
```

In this example, `@each` iterates through the `$theme-colors` map, creating classes like `.bg-primary`, `.bg-secondary`, and `.bg-danger`, applying the corresponding background colors.

@import and @use in Sass

Managing and importing modules is essential for organizing and maintaining CSS code in Sass. The `@import` and `@use` directives are crucial tools in this process, but they have different features and behaviors. Understanding these differences is key to effective code organization.

Differences Between `@import` and `@use`

1. `@import`

- **Deprecated**: The `@import` directive was used in the past to import Sass and CSS files. However, it has been deprecated in favor of `@use` and `@forward` in newer versions of Sass.

- **Imports and Concatenates**: `@import` imports the content of a file and concatenates it into the main file, which can lead to duplication issues and name conflicts.

- **Global Scope**: Variables and mixins imported with `@import` are available globally in the file, which can cause conflicts and maintenance problems.

Example of using `@import`:

```scss
// _variables.scss
$primary-color: #3498db;

// styles.scss
@import 'variables';

.button {
  background-color: $primary-color;
}
```

2. `@use`

- **Module and Encapsulation**: The `@use` directive was introduced to improve module organization and management. It imports a file as a module and encapsulates its contents, avoiding name conflicts and duplication.

- **Namespace by Default**: When using `@use`, module names are encapsulated within a namespace to avoid conflicts. The namespace can be renamed using the `as` option.

- **No Concatenation**: `@use` does not concatenate files. Each module is loaded only once, and its declarations are accessible through the namespace.

Example of using `@use`:

```scss
// _variables.scss

$primary-color: #3498db;


// styles.scss

@use 'variables' as *;
```

```scss
.button {
  background-color: $primary-color; // Directly accessible without namespace
}
```

In this example, `@use 'variables' as *` imports the `_variables.scss` file and makes its variables directly accessible without a namespace.

Organizing Code with Modules

Using modules and the `@use` and `@forward` directives helps organize and maintain CSS code in a more modular and scalable way. Here are some tips for organizing code with these tools:

1. Use `@use` to Import Modules

Use `@use` to import modules and define a namespace to avoid conflicts:

```scss
// _colors.scss
$primary-color: #3498db;

// _typography.scss
@use 'colors';

$font-color: colors.$primary-color;

// main.scss
@use 'colors';
@use 'typography';

.button {
  background-color: colors.$primary-color;
```

```
  color: typography.$font-color;
}
```

In this example, the `_colors.scss` and `_typography.scss` files are imported using `@use`, and their contents are accessible via the namespace.

2. Use `@forward` to Share Modules

The `@forward` directive allows you to re-export modules from one file, making it easier to import them into other files:

```scss
// _index.scss
@forward 'colors';
@forward 'typography';
```

```scss
// main.scss

@use 'index' as *;

.button {
  background-color: $primary-color;
  color: $font-color;
}
```

In this example, the `_index.scss` file uses `@forward` to export the modules from `_colors.scss` and `_typography.scss`, which are then accessible via `@use 'index'`.

Best Practices for Using `@use` and `@import`

1. **Prefer `@use` over `@import`**: `@use` is the recommended directive for new projects because it avoids name conflicts and

duplication. Use `@import` only when maintaining existing code or working with libraries that do not support `@use`.

2. **Utilize Namespaces**: When using `@use`, leverage namespaces to avoid name conflicts and keep the code modular.

3. **Use `@forward` to Re-export Modules**: Use `@forward` to create index files that re-export modules, simplifying imports and improving code organization.

4. **Avoid Duplicate Imports**: With `@use`, modules are imported only once, reducing duplication and conflict issues. Ensure you use `@use` and `@forward` correctly to avoid multiple imports.

5. **Organize Modules by Functionality**: Divide your Sass files into logical modules based on functionality, such as variables, mixins, and styles. This makes the code

more maintainable and modular.

Lists and maps in Sass are powerful tools for managing and manipulating data in a dynamic and modular way. Lists provide a simple way to manage collections of values, while maps allow you to associate keys with structured values. The `@use` directive represents a modern and powerful alternative to `@import`, facilitating module management and improving CSS code organization. Thoughtful use of these features allows you to create more organized, maintainable, and scalable stylesheets, contributing to a more efficient and sustainable CSS development process.

7. Extensions and Placeholders in Sass, Color Management, and Working with CSS Preprocessors

Extensions and placeholders in Sass are advanced tools for CSS management that enable efficient reuse and sharing of styles. Understanding how to use `@extend` and placeholders with `%` is crucial for writing maintainable and well-organized Sass code.

Using `@extend`

The `@extend` directive in Sass allows you to extend the rules of an existing style to a new selector. This is useful for avoiding code duplication and ensuring that multiple selectors share common styles.

Creating Placeholders with `%`

Placeholders are special selectors that begin with `%` and are used exclusively to be extended by other selectors. Placeholders do not generate CSS directly but provide a base of styles that can be extended and reused.

Creating and Using Placeholders

1. **Creating a Placeholder**

```scss
%button-base {
  display: inline-block;
  padding: 10px 20px;
  border-radius: 5px;
  text-align: center;
  cursor: pointer;
}
```

In this example, `%button-base` is a placeholder that defines basic styles for a button. It will not be compiled directly into CSS but can be extended by other selectors.

2. **Extending a Placeholder**

```scss
.button-primary {
  @extend %button-base;
  background-color: #3498db;
  color: white;
}

.button-secondary {
  @extend %button-base;
  background-color: #2ecc71;
  color: white;
}
```

Here, the `.button-primary` and `.button-secondary` classes extend `%button-base`, inheriting all its styles and adding their own. This helps avoid code duplication and maintain consistent styling.

Advantages and Disadvantages of Extending

Advantages

1. **Reduction of Repetition**: By using `@extend` and placeholders, you can avoid duplicating the same CSS rules across different selectors, simplifying code maintenance.

2. **Improved Maintainability**: If you need to update shared styles, you can do so in one place (the placeholder), and the changes will propagate to all selectors that extend that placeholder.

3. **CSS Optimization**: `@extend`

contributes to generating cleaner and more optimized CSS by avoiding the duplication of CSS rules and keeping the code leaner.

Disadvantages

1. **Complexity of Specificity**: The use of `@extend` can complicate the specificity of the generated CSS. This can make it difficult to predict and control which style is applied to an element, especially in complex projects.

2. **Scalability and Readability**: Overusing `@extend` can lead to less readable CSS and harder debugging. This is particularly true if placeholders are extended in many different places, leading to overly complex selectors.

3. **Naming Issues**: If not managed properly, the use of `@extend` can cause naming conflicts, especially in large CSS projects with many selectors extending the same placeholders.

Color Management

Sass offers powerful tools for color manipulation, allowing you to apply color transformations directly within the stylesheet. This is particularly useful for maintaining color consistency and applying dynamic changes to the colors used in the design.

Color Manipulation with Sass

Sass's built-in color functions allow you to modify and combine colors in various ways. The main functions for color manipulation are `lighten`, `darken`, `mix`, and `complement`.

Sass Color Functions

1. **`lighten($color, $amount)`**

   The `lighten` function lightens a color by a

certain amount. The second parameter represents the amount of lightening, expressed as a percentage.

```scss
$base-color: #3498db;

$light-color: lighten($base-color, 20%);


.header {

  background-color: $light-color; // Result: #5dade2

}
```

In this example, `lighten($base-color, 20%)` lightens the base color `#3498db` by 20%, resulting in `#5dade2`.

2. **`darken($color, $amount)`**

The `darken` function darkens a color by a certain amount. Here too, the second parameter is a percentage that determines how dark the color becomes.

```scss
$base-color: #3498db;
$dark-color: darken($base-color, 20%);

.button {
    background-color: $dark-color; // Result: #2980b9
}
```

In this example, `darken($base-color, 20%)` darkens the base color `#3498db` by 20%, resulting in `#2980b9`.

3. **`mix($color1, $color2, $weight)`**

The `mix` function blends two colors with a given weight. The third parameter represents the weight of the first color relative to the second, expressed as a percentage.

```scss
$color1: #3498db;

$color2: #2ecc71;

$mixed-color: mix($color1, $color2, 50%);


.card {

  background-color: $mixed-color; // Result: #66c1d0

}
```

In this example, `mix($color1, $color2, 50%)` blends the colors `#3498db` and `#2ecc71` in equal proportions, resulting in an intermediate color `#66c1d0`.

4. **`complement($color)`**

The `complement` function returns the complementary color of a given color. The complementary color is the opposite of the color on the color wheel.

```scss
$base-color: #3498db;

$complement-color: complement($base-color);

.footer {
  background-color: $complement-color; // Result: #e74c3c
}
```

In this example, `complement($base-color)` returns the complementary color of

`#3498db`, which is `#e74c3c`.

Working with CSS Preprocessors

Integrating Sass with build tools like Gulp and Webpack is crucial for a modern and automated workflow in CSS management. Properly configuring build settings helps optimize the CSS development and production process.

Sass Integration with Build Tools

1. Gulp

Gulp is a JavaScript task runner that can be used to automate the compilation of Sass into CSS. Setting up Gulp for Sass involves installing the necessary packages and creating a `gulpfile.js` configuration file.

Example of Gulp Configuration with Sass

1. **Installing the Packages**

   ```bash
   npm install gulp gulp-sass sass --save-dev
   ```

2. **Creating a `gulpfile.js`**

   ```javascript
   const gulp = require('gulp');
   const sass = require('gulp-sass')(require('sass'));

   function compileSass() {
     return gulp.src('src/scss/**/*.scss') // Path to Sass files
       .pipe(sass().on('error', sass.logError))
   ```

```
    .pipe(gulp.dest('dist/css'));  // Destination for compiled files

}


function watch() {

  gulp.watch('src/scss/**/*.scss', compileSass);  // Watches for changes in Sass files

}


  exports.default = gulp.series(compileSass, watch);

```

In this example, `gulp-sass` is used to compile Sass files and save the resulting CSS in the `dist/css` folder. The `watch` function monitors changes in `.scss` files and automatically recompiles them when modified.

2. Webpack

Webpack is a module bundler that can handle Sass compilation using the appropriate loaders. Setting up Webpack for Sass requires installing the necessary packages and configuring the `webpack.config.js` file.

Example of Webpack Configuration with Sass

1. **Installing the Packages**

```bash
npm install webpack webpack-cli sass sass-loader css-loader --save-dev
```

2. **Creating a `webpack.config.js`**

```javascript
const path = require('path');

module.exports = {
  entry: './src/index.js', // Entry file
  output: {
    filename: 'bundle.js',
    path: path.resolve(__dirname, 'dist'),
  },
  module: {
    rules: [
      {
        test: /\.scss$/,
        use: [
          'style-loader', // Injects CSS into the DOM
          'css-loader',   // Handles CSS
          'sass-loader',  // Compiles Sass to CSS
```

```
            ],
          },
        ],
      },
    };
    ```

In this example, `sass-loader` compiles Sass into CSS, `css-loader` handles the CSS, and `style-loader` injects the compiled CSS into the DOM.

Compilation Settings Configuration

Configuring Sass compilation settings depends on the development environment and the tools used. Here are some important aspects to consider:

1. **Input and Output Paths**

Define the paths for input files (where your `.scss` files are located) and output files (where the compiled CSS files will be saved). This is crucial to ensure that files are compiled to the desired location.

2. **Compilation Options**

Configure compilation options, such as the output mode (production or development), error handling, and file mapping options (source maps). Source maps are useful for debugging, as they allow mapping the compiled CSS to the original Sass files.

3. **Watch Mode**

Enable watch mode to automatically recompile Sass files whenever they are modified. This speeds up the workflow during development.

4. **File Concatenation**

Consider whether you want to concatenate all compiled CSS files into a single file. This is often done to reduce the number of HTTP requests made by the browser, improving performance.

8. Advanced Techniques in Sass

Sass is a powerful CSS preprocessor that not only simplifies the writing and management of CSS but also offers a range of advanced techniques to improve productivity and code maintainability. These techniques include conditional statements, loops, and grouping variables into unique structures. Below, we will explore these techniques in detail and provide practical examples of how they can be used in a complete project.

Conditional Statements in Sass

Conditional statements in Sass are used to apply styles based on certain conditions. These can be useful for managing different styles for various situations, such as dark and light themes or specific changes for different devices.

Using `@if` and `@else`

Sass offers the `@if` directive to execute blocks of CSS code based on conditions. You can also use `@else` to handle alternative cases.

Example of Conditional Statements

```scss
$theme: dark;

.button {
  @if $theme == light {
    background-color: #fff;
    color: #000;
  } @else if $theme == dark {
    background-color: #333;
    color: #fff;
  } @else {
```

```
    background-color: #ccc;

    color: #000;

  }
}
```

In this example, the button's background and text colors change based on the value of the `$theme` variable. If `$theme` is `light`, a light color scheme is applied; if it is `dark`, a dark color scheme is applied. If `$theme` doesn't match either option, a default color scheme is applied.

Using `@each` and `@for` to Manage Conditions

In addition to `@if`, you can combine conditional statements with loops to create dynamic styles based on arrays or ranges of values.

Example of Loops with Conditions

```scss
$colors: (primary: #3498db, secondary: #2ecc71, danger: #e74c3c);

.button {
  @each $name, $color in $colors {
    &.#{$name} {
      background-color: $color;
      color: #fff;
    }
  }
}
```

In this example, `@each` iterates over a color map, creating `.primary`, `.secondary`, and

`.danger` classes with their respective background colors.

Looping in Sass

Loops in Sass allow you to perform repetitive operations and generate CSS dynamically. Sass supports several loop structures, including `@for`, `@each`, and `@while`.

Using `@for`

The `@for` directive is useful for generating styles based on numerical ranges.

Example of a `@for` Loop

```scss
@for $i from 1 through 5 {
  .item-#{$i} {
```

```
    width: 20px * $i;
    margin-right: 10px;
  }
}
```

In this example, `@for` generates classes `.item-1`, `.item-2`, `.item-3`, and so on, with increasing widths.

Using `@each`

The `@each` directive iterates over collections like lists and maps.

Example of an `@each` Loop with Lists

```scss
$sizes: (small, medium, large);
```

```
@each $size in $sizes {
  .box-#{$size} {
    width: if($size == small, 100px, if($size == medium, 200px, 300px));
    height: 100px;
  }
}
```

In this example, `@each` creates `.box-small`, `.box-medium`, and `.box-large` classes with different widths based on the size.

Using `@while`

The `@while` directive is used for condition-based loops.

Example of a `@while` Loop

```scss
$i: 1;

@while $i <= 5 {
  .item-#{$i} {
    width: 20px * $i;
    margin-right: 10px;
  }
  $i: $i + 1;
}
```

In this example, `@while` creates classes `.item-1` through `.item-5`, similar to the `@for` example, but using conditional logic.

Grouping Variables into a Single Structure

Organizing variables into a single structure like a map or object allows you to manage data more efficiently and centrally. This approach makes it easier to modify and maintain the code.

Creating Variable Maps

Maps in Sass are useful for grouping related variables into a single structure.

Example of a Variable Map

```scss
$theme: (
  primary-color: #3498db,
  secondary-color: #2ecc71,
  font-color: #333,
  background-color: #fff
);
```

```scss
.button {

  background-color: map-get($theme, primary-color);

  color: map-get($theme, font-color);

}


.card {

  background-color: map-get($theme, background-color);

  border: 1px solid map-get($theme, primary-color);

}
```

In this example, a `$theme` map collects color and style variables, and `map-get` is used to retrieve values within the CSS rules.

Using Variables for Dynamic Themes

Maps can also be used to manage dynamic themes or complex configurations.

Example of a Dynamic Theme

```scss
$themes: (
  light: (
    background: #fff,
    color: #000
  ),
  dark: (
    background: #333,
    color: #fff
  )
);
```

```
$selected-theme: light;

body {
  background-color: map-get(map-get($themes, $selected-theme), background);
  color: map-get(map-get($themes, $selected-theme), color);
}
```

In this example, the `$themes` map manages different themes, and the `$selected-theme` variable determines which theme to apply.

Practical Examples

To demonstrate the use of advanced Sass techniques, consider a complete application that uses conditional statements, loops, and variable maps to manage a theme and dynamic styles.

Complete Project: Theme System for a Dashboard

Imagine creating a theme system for a dashboard that supports light and dark themes. We will use Sass to manage color variables, conditional styles, and loops to generate dynamic components.

Project Structure

```
/src
  /scss
    _variables.scss
    _mixins.scss
    _components.scss
    main.scss
```

`_variables.scss` File

```scss
$themes: (
  light: (
    background: #fff,
    text: #000,
    primary: #3498db,
    secondary: #2ecc71
  ),
  dark: (
    background: #333,
    text: #fff,
    primary: #2980b9,
    secondary: #27ae60
  )
);
```

```scss
$selected-theme: light;
```

`_mixins.scss` File

```scss
@mixin theme($theme-name) {
  $theme: map-get($themes, $theme-name);

  background-color: map-get($theme, background);
  color: map-get($theme, text);

  .button {
    background-color: map-get($theme, primary);
    color: map-get($theme, text);
  }
```

```
  .card {
    border: 1px solid map-get($theme, primary);
  }
}
```

`_components.scss` File

```scss
@import 'variables';
@import 'mixins';

body {
  @include theme($selected-theme);
}

.card {
```

```
  width: 100%;
  padding: 20px;
  margin: 10px 0;
}


.button {
  display: inline-block;
  padding: 10px 20px;
  border-radius: 5px;
  cursor: pointer;
}
```

`main.scss` File

```scss
@import 'components';
```

Example Details

- **Theme Variables**: The theme variables are grouped into a `$themes` map, which includes options for `light` and `dark`. The `$selected-theme` variable is used to apply the currently selected theme.

- **Theme Mixin**: The `theme` mixin applies styles based on the selected theme, using `map-get` to access the theme variable values.

- **Dynamic Components**: The `.card` and `.button` classes

are defined with general styles, but specific styles like background colors and borders are dynamically managed by the `theme` mixin.

Advanced techniques in Sass, such as conditional statements, loops, and grouping variables into unique structures, provide powerful tools to manage and optimize your stylesheets. By using these techniques, you can create more dynamic, modular, and maintainable CSS. The practical example of a theme system for a dashboard demonstrates how to combine these techniques to create a complete and well-organized application. These advanced Sass tools significantly enhance productivity and the quality of CSS code, making the development process more efficient and scalable.

Index

1. Introduction pg.4

2. Basic Concepts pg.23

3. Variables in Sass pg.46

4. Nesting, Mixins in Sass pg.69

5. Functions and Operators pg.89

6. Lists and Maps in Sass, and @import and @use pg.107

7. Extensions and Placeholders in Sass, Color Management, and Working with CSS Preprocessors pg.125

8.Advanced Techniques in Sass pg.143

www.ingramcontent.com/pod-product-compliance
Lightning Source LLC
Chambersburg PA
CBHW052204220526
45471CB00004B/1812